OLD SOUTH

MALLARD
PRESS

Photography
FPG International
Odyssey Publishing Ltd

Photo Editor
Annette Lerner

MALLARD PRESS

An imprint of BDD Promotional
Book Company Inc., 666 Fifth
Avenue, New York, NY 10103

Mallard Press and its
accompanying design and logo are
trademarks of BDD Promotional
Book Company, Inc.

Color separations by Advance
Laser Graphic Arts, Hong Kong.

Printed and bound
in Hong Kong.

ISBN 0-7924-5480-1

*Previous pages: a Civil War
reenactment in the South. Right:
Rock Bridge Canyon, Alabama.*

No matter what anyone predicts for the future of the New South, one thing's for sure: there'll always be an Old South. For proof, you don't have to look any further than the barefoot kid out squirrel hunting with a fine-looking rifle.

He's proud to tell you that it's the gun his Grandpappy carried into battle during the War between the States. It doesn't look like an antique, though, and the barrel is shorter than the kind they used in those days. That's because his daddy fitted a new one. The stock isn't very old-looking either; his Grandpappy made that a few years ago. And if the stock is handmade, the lock was obviously made by machine, and not too long ago at that. But does all that make it a new rifle? Not on your life! As far as the boy is concerned, it's the same gun that picked off Yankees at the second battle of Bull Run.

The scars of war have long since healed as far as the younger generation is concerned, but in the South there is a respect for the past that is unique in America, and it is as munch a part of the fabric of life as television and shopping malls.

And if shopping malls have become the great social centers in the America of the '90s, it's not a new phenomenon in the South, where the local emporium has been, after the churches, the gathering place of choice for two centuries. You could buy anything in those general stores: high-top shoes with a free pocket knife mounted on the side, a new pair of jeans twice a years, and a calico frock for your little sister. A man could find a bottle of cologne to make him smell prettier than the flowers in May, and if its magic worked just right, he could buy a wedding ring there, too. And his new bride could find all the yard goods she needed to make a proper dress to wear when the circuit-riding preacher passed through and hitched them up. It could all be bought on credit against the day the crops came in, and to help that day along every tool a man could want, from a plow to a scythe, could be found down at the general store.

But something more important could also be found there. When the weather was bad and they couldn't work in their fields, farm families gathered from miles around to share each other's company on the store's front porch, or inside, around its wood stove. They'd play checkers, tell tall tales and swap gossip. When an election was coming up the politicians would join them there, at other times they'd debate the fine points of scripture, and try to settle the question of whether the Methodists or the Baptists had the right ideas.

Most of the crossroads stores have gone the way of the horse and buggy. But if they've got paved roads now, and telephones and electric lights, not to mention shopping malls, the South remembers a time when no one could have predicted that such things would ever exist. And the memories are fond ones.

In the mind's eye the Old South is a land of soft-spoken gentlemen on horseback and beautiful women in crinolines wandering through rose gardens. It is a place of elegant mansions, usually white and embellished with Greek Revival elements; the land of the yeoman farmer in whose hands, Thomas Jefferson felt, rested the future of America. Their fences may have sagged, and their houses might have been left unpainted, but their barns were full most winters and, in spite of the images of prosperous plantations, their farms were the backbone of the Old South. And if they weren't rich, it's a myth and an injustice to lump them all together as "poor whites."

The ways of the Old South were American before they were Southern. Most of the people who settled there were second and third generation native-born Americans, whose folkways were home-grown and not the remembered ways of a foreign country. The pattern of family pride and clan loyalties, of honor and a love of traditional values that still exists in the New South is as close as the rest of America can get to its own frontier roots. Fortunately for all of us it is all still there, because the more the New South changes, the more the Old South stays the same.

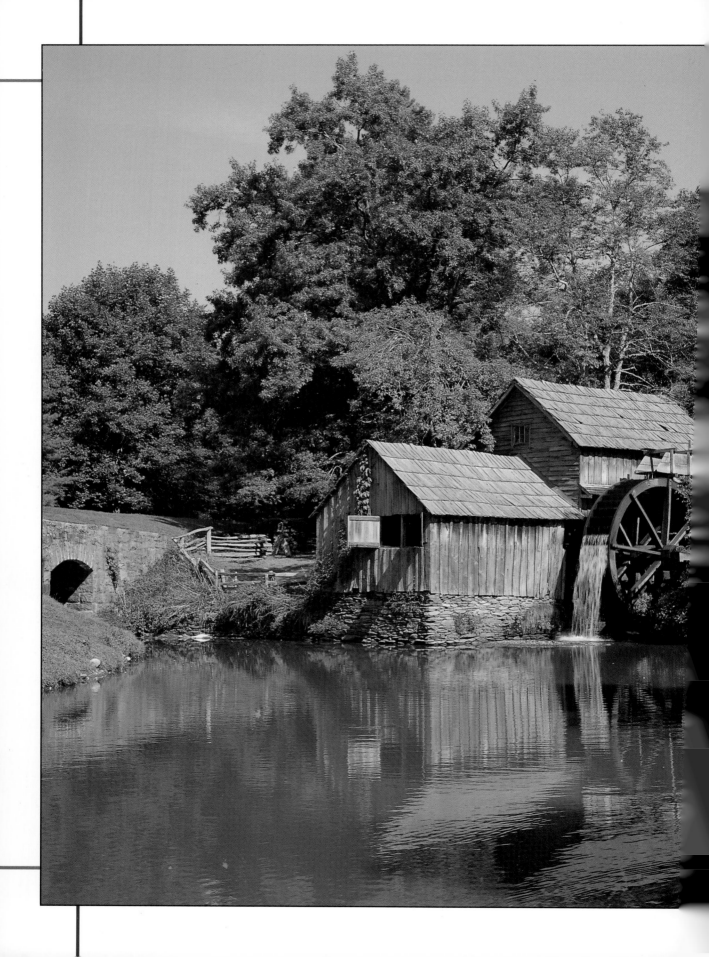

Mabry Mill (left) lies along the Blue Ridge Parkway in southwest Virginia, the highland pioneer country of Daniel Boone's Wilderness Road, the Trail of the Lonesome Pine and the legends of the Hatfields and McCoys. The power it generated ran a sawmill and a gristmill for the use of local farmers. Above: the Timson House, Colonial Williamsburg, Virginia. Williamsburg was founded in 1699 to replace Jamestown as colonial capital of Virginia. Governor Francis Nicholson designed this gracious, uncramped town on the basis of houses with half-acre lots.

Monticello (below), begun in 1769, was the home of Thomas Jefferson (left). Jefferson was an architect by profession, and designed Monticello to an "Age of Reason" style, incorporating aspects of Greek architecture. The Governor's Palace (facing page) was constructed when Colonial Williamsburg became Virginia's second state capital. Patrick Henry once said: "Caesar had his Brutus, Charles I his Cromwell, and George III …" he was interrupted at this point with cries of "treason! treason!" to finish with "may profit by their example." The King evidently did not and Patrick Henry, as independent Virginia's first state governor, moved into the palace in 1776, succeeded by Thomas Jefferson in 1779.

Above: Prince Street in Old Town Alexandria, Virginia. George Washington had a town house built in this tobacco port. In fact in 1748, when he was a teenager, he was one of the surveyors who laid out the grid of Alexandria's streets. However his heart belonged to his other Virginia home, about which he said: "No estate in United America is more pleasantly situated than Mount Vernon" (right).

Facing page: Great Falls on the Potomac River, Virginia (these pages). Above: Chesapeake Bay Beach, and (right) commemorative firing of cannon in Petersburg National Battlefield, the scene of a seige lasting over nine months, beginning in June 1864, between the forces of Union General Ulysses S. Grant and Confederate General Robert E. Lee. The series of battles that summer contributed to the defeat of the South and Lee's surrender at Appomattox Court House on April 9, 1865.

Facing page: downtown Memphis, Tennessee (these pages). Memphis sprang up in 1818 as a trading outpost. Today it is best known for its musicians, among them Elvis Presley and W.C. Handy, who developed his masterpieces "Memphis Blues" and "St. Louis Blues" in the honky-tonks of Beale Street.

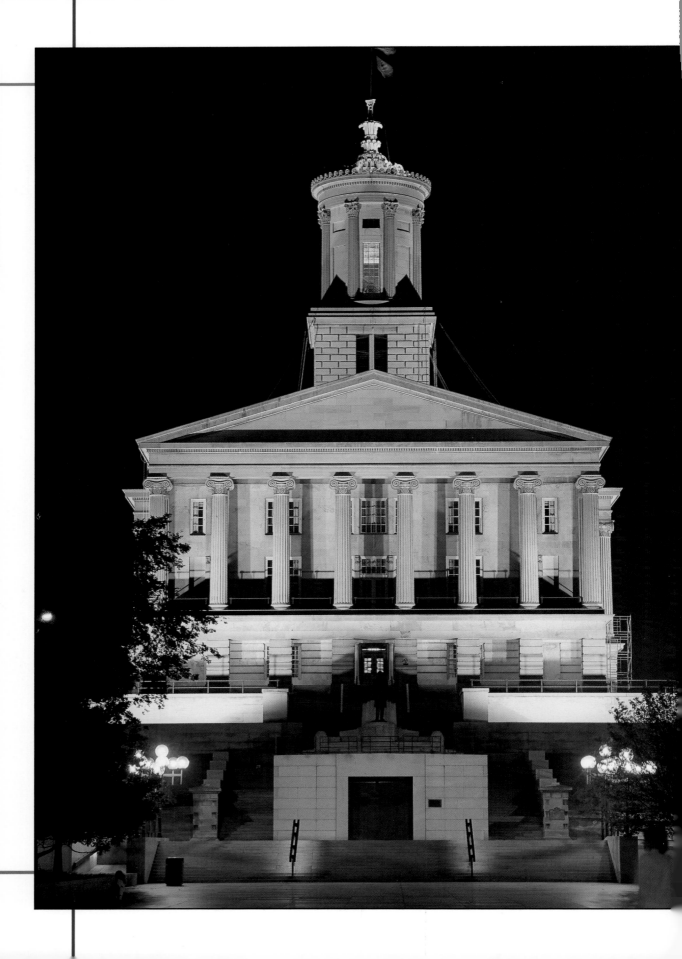

Facing page: the 1859 State Capitol, Nashville, and (above) Pickwick Landing. Left: a volunteer soldier dressed as he would have been in February 1862 in Fort Donelson National Military Park, Tennessee (these pages), the Volunteer State.

Hanging Rock State Park, west of Danbury in North Carolina, covers more than 5,000 acres of great natural beauty in the Sauratown Mountains.

Left: Fontana Lake in the Smoky Mountains of North Carolina. Below: the 182-foot-tall steeple of St. Michael's Church, the oldest church building in Charleston, South Carolina. It looks very like London's St. Martin-in-the-Fields and was probably designed by the same architect, James Gibbs. This London connection exercised a strong pull on its bells, which were originally shipped over from England in 1764; shipped back as spoils during the War of Independence; returned later, and, during the Civil War, shipped to England once again for recasting.

Below: Cypress Gardens, Charleston (left), South Carolina (these pages). Facing page: the Adventure is a replica of a seventeenth-century trading ketch at historic Charles Towne Landing on the Ashley River. This site was where the original Charles Towne settlement was established in 1670. It was chosen for its seclusion; the English colonists thought they would evade both Spaniards and pirates there. Eventually they moved to the city's present location, but some of the original fortifications still stand.

In 1886, a group of millionaires formed the Jekyll Island Club and bought the island for $125,000. Goulds, Pulitzers, Rockerfellers, Morgans and Astors built winter "cottages" there. However, the club later declined and was dissolved in 1947. Left: Rockerfeller's twenty-five-room "cottage," and (right) the Club House, Jekyll Island. Christ Church (below) in Frederica, St. Simon's Island, also off Georgia, was built in 1820 on what may have been the site on which, in 1776, John and Charles Wesley preached to the first congregation.

A view from the Appalachian Highway near the Blue Ridge Mountains in Georgia.

Facing page: the gilded dome of Atlanta's State Capitol Building, surmounted by Liberty holding her torch 258 feet above the city. The Capitol was dedicated on July 4, 1889. Above: the carved granite of Stone Mountain, east of Atlanta, Georgia (these pages). The sculpture is of Confederate President Jefferson Davis, and generals Robert E. Lee and "Stonewall" Jackson mounted on their horses. Commissioned in 1916 by the Daughters of the Confederacy, it was finished in 1970, over fifty years and three sculptors later. The design and original work was done by Gutzon Borglum, who was responsible for Mount Rushmore. However, he resigned in 1924 and destroyed his models over a disagreement with the sponsors. Right: the ornate balustrade of a home in Savannah.

The Civil War left an indelible imprint on the consciousness of the South.
Some states never recovered their former economic stature and others,
though prosperous again, such as Georgia (these pages), still remember
the Civil War in reenactments involving both armies, Union (left) and
Confederate, and in monuments such as the Confederate Memorial
(above) in Savannah's Forsythe Park. Savannah was relatively
unscathed by the war, capitulating to General Sherman's seige without
armed conflict on December 22, 1864.

Walt Disney World (facing page) opened near Orlando, Florida in 1971. Right: air-plants growing like skirts on cypress trees in Everglades National Park. The park was established in 1947 to protect 2,120 square miles of Florida's subtropical wilderness and the wildlife, including very rare species, which it supports.

Jefferson Davis was sworn in as President of the Confederacy at Alabama's State Capitol (facing page), Montgomery, in February 1861. Right: the Confederate Monument, also in Montgomery. Oakleigh (below), a beautiful antebellum home in Mobile, Alabama, took cotton broker James Roper, who designed the house himself, five years to build, finally reaching completion in 1838. It is built of bricks hand-made using clay which came from a pit on the estate. The sunken garden is said to occupy the area of the old clay pit.

Longwood, Dr. Haller Nutt's octagonal home, near Natchez, Mississippi. This beautifully ornate house is empty – construction was interrupted by the Civil War.

Left: Stanton Hall, Natchez, Mississippi (these pages). Frederick Stanton completed the house in 1858 and called it "Belfast," in memory of his homeland, Ireland. He died a few months later and his name for the house didn't stick. Locals referred to it as Stanton Hall. Below: Linden, an antebellum mansion near Natchez, which featured in the famous movie Gone with the Wind. Happily it didn't vanish with the way of life it represented in the chaos that followed the Civil War. Linden arose from a two-storied cottage around 1792, and in 1818 Thomas B. Reed, Mississippi's first U.S. senator, bought it. Facing page: De Soto Lake in Coahoma County.

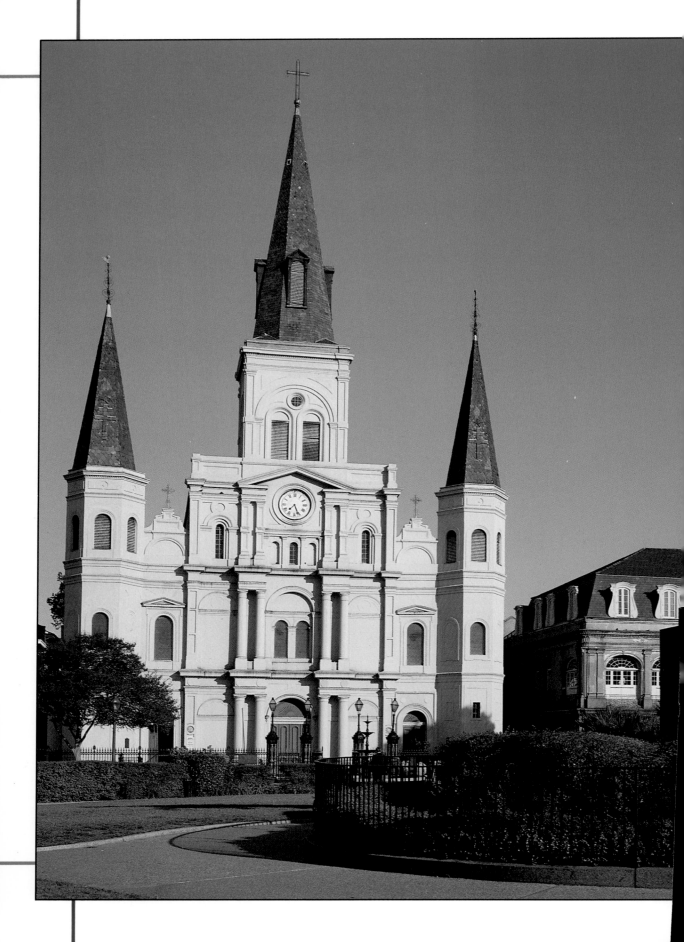

THE UNION MUST
AND
SHALL BE PRESERVED

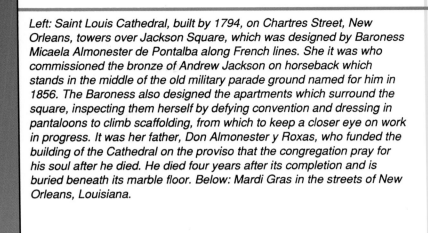

Left: Saint Louis Cathedral, built by 1794, on Chartres Street, New Orleans, towers over Jackson Square, which was designed by Baroness Micaela Almonester de Pontalba along French lines. She it was who commissioned the bronze of Andrew Jackson on horseback which stands in the middle of the old military parade ground named for him in 1856. The Baroness also designed the apartments which surround the square, inspecting them herself by defying convention and dressing in pantaloons to climb scaffolding, from which to keep a closer eye on work in progress. It was her father, Don Almonester y Roxas, who funded the building of the Cathedral on the proviso that the congregation pray for his soul after he died. He died four years after its completion and is buried beneath its marble floor. Below: Mardi Gras in the streets of New Orleans, Louisiana.

The Louisiana steamer Natchez *plies the waters of the Mississippi at New Orleans, flying the flags of all the countries to have had an interest in New Orleans.*

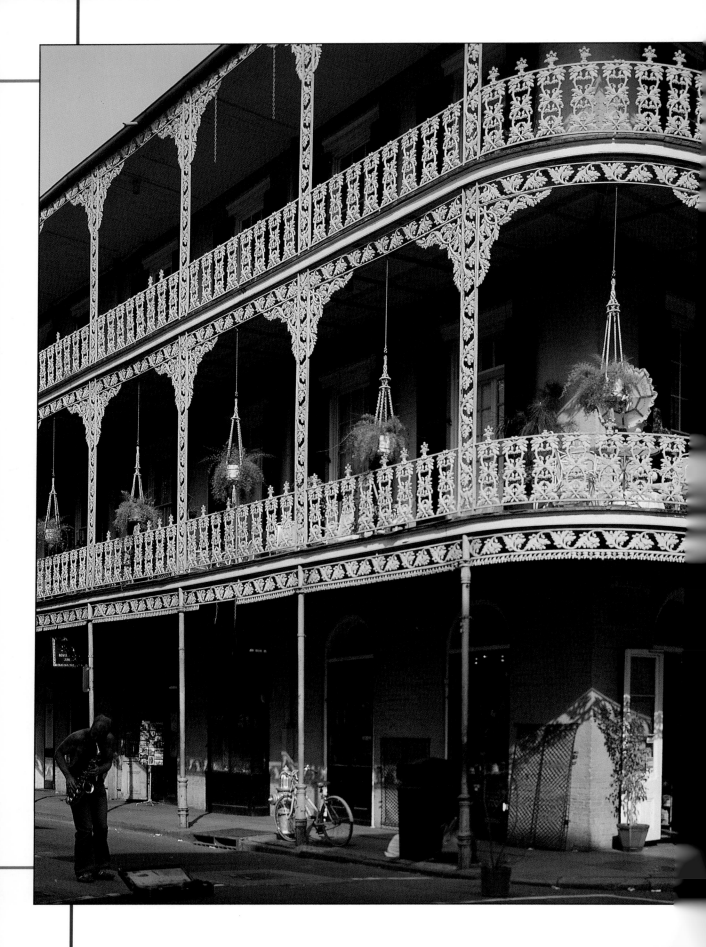

The iron lace of the balconies on 700 Royal Street (facing page), built in 1835 by Jean LaBrance in the Vieux Carré of New Orleans, consists of an intricate pattern of acorns and twining oak leaves. Ardoyne (above), built in 1900 near Houma, Louisiana (these pages), was copied from a picture of a Scottish castle. This Victorian house has twenty-one rooms, all with sixteen-foot-high ceilings. Oak Alley Plantation (left), Vacherie, takes its name from the avenue of live oaks that were already 100 years old when the house was built in 1850. Overleaf: the russets of Virginia in the fall.